Omn...
H...

Craig Coyle

Copyright © 2024 Craig Coyle
All rights reserved
ISBN: 9798326667403

## Contents

1. Ommatidia — p.5
2. Scivias — p.15
3. In Consequence of a son — p.26

OMMATIDIA

Who or what is writing this?
Again he tries
to read his own eyesight.


On the concrete wall:
my shadow.
Just one thing more in this world


My shadow
is
the evidence.


Creature. Out
of what?
From where?


Ego blooms,
like
a bruise.


Ground-Zero hush
that photographs
the bones of the soul.


Spiral staircase
centred
on an ion.


Where the membrane
flares to ash
and, blinking, open-mouthed, we receive.

Adrenalin supernova
fuelled by
the grains of our dust!


Gather weapons,
and brood
on your restoration.


Ego: magnet
that
repels itself.


Floor of the mind. Survivors
signal
through the Foraminifera.


Snowfall. Fat world
haunted
by famished clerks.


Blackbird. Peering
through his microscope,
making notes.


Snow-silence...angry
car-faces
drive past in the direction I just came from.


There! My face reflected
in the glass
of a passing car!

Marshmallow slo-mo
dreamslide
towards a very hard tree!


Look at me, in
my Volkswagen
monster-mask!


Leaf-storm!
Envious
of the fat.


Leaf-storm! Laughing,
I shadow-box
dead trees.


Under streetlamps, our neighbours
Chrysler
with its metal fish-face.


Preserved by the retina
the lightbulb's
bones


On the retina:
Zig-zags.
Fireflies on the verge of cuneiform.


We are flies! We are flies!
Electron detailing
in the eye of the Mantis, watching.

Cape Cod, 1971. Wave bye-bye to the camera....
Childhood
encased in silence.


The click of a flea
in a quiet room.
Truly, I am hunted by things that are glossy and implacable.


Electron micrograph of speech:
moonscape
in which the virus moves, in search of our best intentions.


Full moon. Willow trees
animate
with waterfall and skeleton.

How real the World
with its
hands of bone.


In a splinter of glass
the shining
impersonality of light.


Go towards the light
fruitfly! Towards
the light!


Fruitfly, his
madness deepening
in the mirror.

I read the final
bone, and
try to make an answer.


In the mirror: lovingly he adjusts
the ego-machine's
epiphenomena.


Who am I?
        What am I?
Wiggling
a loose screw.


Corkscrew inspection!
He examines
the drill sample.


Blue-black beetle:
sun's
lightswitch.


Head disperses.....!
Beetle
survives the blast.


And the bare
patch of temple-earth
on which it crawls.


Cough! Examine the source
before
it closes over!

Who am I?
        What am I?
He examines each word
for fingerprints.


With bloody fingernails he edges
towards
the event horizon

Look at this! He sucks
and blows
at the same time!


3am. He suddenly realises
he is the eye
of Struthiomimus.


He shouts so hard
his spit wets my face.
Who or What is he shouting at?


Who or What is asking this question?
The lense
tries to read the eye.


He tries to think microscopically,
to be free
of his own mass.


The point
hungers
towards ignition.

Who am I?
        What am I?
Mind's
steady snowfall…

At the scene of the crime:
the underside of your own
footprint.


Sneeze! A momentary
rent
in the veil.


Who am I?
        What am I?
Beat me,
I'm a pinata.


On the concrete path this morning,
a dead hatchling with it's
veinous cranium.


It looks as if
its eyes
had not yet unsealed.


The light illuminates it
in great detail.
Look: pores, veins, the unfeathered wing stumps.


On my back, too,
the unfeathered
wing stumps.

Rotate me like a jewel. The light
will always snag
on a flaw.


I sit on a chair
in a cold room, at 5.47 am,
writing this.


[Who or What is writing this?]
Arse bones
aching on a hard chair.


Who am I?
           What am I?
Word-flies
circling the light.


Silence...yet still this background fizz:
the effervescence
of mystical chemicals.


Cataracts of serotonin,
fumaroles
of dopamine!


Catalytic, alert and
laughing
in this World.


August. Windowsill
hot beneath his elbows.
Breathe in
         Breathe out

With bloody fingers
he gropes
for the lightswitch.


Who am I?
          What am I?
The mirrored
intestine.


In its jewelled vestments
born of the meat of this world:
the adjective.


I advance, loosening
like river foam
or a creature made of Alka Seltzer.


In the eyepiece: viscous
microscopic world.
But our mouths disintegrate even as we cry in wonder.


Even so, choreiform butterflies
wobble onwards
with their busted gyroscopes.


Cabbage White: fragile dignity
dogged at the heels
by life's lopsided wobble.


Dying even as I unhook it:
zinc trout, cold,
ontology's monstrance.

Last night, Lord, I saw a dead tree signified
in a field of lightning, as if
You were negating Yourself.


On the rim of comprehension: a thread
of gold,
metaphysical:


a language
unable
to sunrise.


Frosty morning.
cows
fart steam.

SCIVIAS

Who am I?
        What am I?
The day slides by outside:
a cold and distant plaque of light and noise.


I was running.
A flower!
I hurtled past it along an adrenalin corridor.


Snowdrop
photography of an instant
clear, real


Reality-coordinate:
snowdrop's
magnesium bell.


The fly-cobra
that danced in front of me at twenty fathoms
Breathe in
        Breathe out


Preserved by the retina
the lightbulb's
bones


Wet pebble, evening star:
small pieces
of a high-fidelity world.

What luck
my teeth deflected
        the bee!


Yawning, the dog
reveals
a Romanesque interior.


Granular earth
patrolled
by mighty-headed ants.


Odours of earth
released
by the impact of raindrops.


Leaf-shadow
inscribed on stone:
sunreality.


Querying
decapitated torso
Breathe in
        Breathe out


In the mirror: an iris,
etched there
by lysergic acid diethylamide.


Where mind
sinks below the threshold of its neurons
        the blue

Inward detonation!
Where we eavesdrop and lipread
as if through a microscope.


Ground-Zero hush
that photographs
the bones of the soul.


Spiral staircase
centred
on an ion.


Where the membrane
flares to ash
and, blinking, open-mouthed, we receive.


In its jewelled vestments
born of the meat of this world:
the adjective.


Wren's egg: slow growth
of creature
in its bubble of world.


My inflated shadow
terrorises
my meagre prayer, as if across a cold, calcium sky.


A glimpsed Goldfinch
releases this
from the ego-machine!

Where mind
rises along a fractal curve
                      and dawns


At the brittle horizon:
our dead,
with their infinitesimal gestures.


Petroleum meadows.
Through a heat-warp
an ascension of larks.


Gripping between his hands
the branches of two trees
he attempts to electrocute himself.


The relentless growth of trees:
new fuel
for the bonefire.


Even a crude spade
augments
the work of creation.


Tree gears gripping the earth, the earth
revolves
in her seasons.


Adrenalin supernova
fuelled by
the grains of our dust!

Who am I?
        What am I?
Fractal galleries
of Self…


Small music at the root of the breath!
3 am
amplification.


October. Trees
disintegrating
in a cold wind.

Mighty sky of depth and stars
regard me, here,
thin-armed and squeaky voiced.


As if Sirius was its tool
silence engraves
across a clear sensorium.


Big sky. Little me.
My cilia
stir in the wind.


So cold the Quince tree, now it is November.
My spine
recognises it.


Boneless mind, rejoice!
Those peristaltic
rivers of limestone…

Wheeeeeeeeeeeeeeeeeeeeeeeeeeeeeeeeeeeeeeee.........!
Time-lapse
review of life.


Woodgrain, teacup, rise up
renewed,
hard and detailed, beyond my jurisdiction.


Nuclear implosive teacup
strengthening
into itself.


Like a knuckle
the mind,
under a migraine's glistening ceiling.


Lightning, ragged landscape. Where the demiurge
cuts shapes
with a chainsaw.


There it is! My Tonka truck,
frozen into
memory's floor.


The luminous plaque of the Insect-O-cutor
coolly imbues
the nearby willow.


All night long, the pop
and sizzle
of exoskelatanous insects.

A rain of parts…where grasses
crunch
underfoot.


Stitching a marshmallow
into the grass:
threads of fungi.


Cracked, golden interior
of the willow
hit by lightning!


Attic floorboards spiced
with dust…gone!
How upright and offices I have become!


Full moon. Willow trees
animate
with waterfall and skeleton.


Under streetlamps, our neighbours
Chrysler
with its metal fish-face.


On the retina:
zig-zags.
Fireflies on the verge of cuneiform.


Speeded-up crowds
on Saint Peter's Square: they shimmer
like rain.

On the floor of the Duomo:
migratory
plates of shadow.


Dead fox
with frosted corneas, we pass
each other in a field.


In the hot glare of the desk-lamp:
slow plunge
of a dust speck.


Seen in a monstrance of sunlight
a frosted tree
makes a meaning. I am illiterate.


On the darkening lawn
a blackbird
reads the grass.


Dead pig hanging
from a butchers hook. It, too, is part of
the world-mobile.


Butcher's shop: dead chickens dangling
from their snapped
chains of being.


Dead leaves disperse…
Are we just nourishing
our spines?

A blackbird at dawn
presents itself
as a liquid.


On the forest path: a bird's
intact skeleton.
Daylight a slow Hiroshima.


In the wood of the threshold:
bullet holes
of Spirochaeta Pallida.


Dry, granular snow
sizzles
in the fir tree.


Distant snowhills:
eternity's
contingent ceramics.


Ignoring the face which is me
a cold wind
communes with my skull.


January. A cold wind
enhances
my hard skull.


Seen from the Intercity train at night:
the lit interiors
of other people's homes.

In the eye of the whirlwind:
an Act's
interior, close up.


At the graveside:
rows of polished shoes,
hard-soled.


World-mountain of iron.
Blood on
my forehead.


Vale of Leven cemetery.
Polished gravestones
wink in the passing lights of cars.


Ribonucleic birdsong!
An alien hermeneutic
infects me.


Uspstreet, a dog's barking
amplified
in a concrete stairwell.


Hard sheets of sound
blank out
the mouthed prayer.


He reinterprets himself,
thinly reflected
in storm windows.

The breath, boxed
in warm timber, where it hides
under Anna's porch.

IN CONSEQUENCE OF A SON

He was born on 26th June 1999 at 0255am:
a baby boy
fuelled by blue magnesium.


He teaches me that immortality is a matter of perspective: I look like him,
he looks like my father.


He is the silver lining
on a cloud
of unknowing,


A refinement
of the law
of identity:


His shadow
is edged
with tool-steel.


His cry is a freshly-created
dimension
of space,


a
rose,
Mandelbrotian


He will carry with him 188 days of the 20th century
into the 21st,
like an achilles heel.

Or a tattoo:
188.
He will survive though his grandfather did not.


The clear silence of his gaze
is the view
from Ground Zero.


I call him my son, but in truth I do not even know what we are!
I thank
the darkness:


I have been
gifted
responsibility.


I play him the 6$^{th}$ Suite for Unaccompanied Cello, the one in which God replies to Bach.
To remind him
of Home.


Judging by the expressions which bubble across his face
he is still positioning himself
in the chain of being.


2.33 am: the self attenuates
in answer
to his cry.


My bony hands assisted at the Deposition, dug trench latrines at Birkenau.
Now they warm
his bottle.

God writes indecipherably and for no one on the interior
walls of a conch shell, as a mark of authenticity.
He also made my sons'
fingernails.


And his irises:
like cross-sectional slices of pure summer sky
arrayed in calm surprise.


In a corner of our livingroom
his quiet breathing
paves a chancel.


When he frowns
he looks like
Eisenhower.


He is our 'little angel', stitched
into the fabric of this world
by a length of gut.


He lies wriggling
on his first crucifix:
the ileum.


I took him to visit his great grandmother in the hospital in
which, just 2 years ago, his grandfather died.
Why are 3,500,000,000 years
not enough?


It worries me that everything I know is of the 20th century,
as if I am an ancestor of his
instead of his father.

Sometimes he cries
because he hears himself
crying.


His newness
bends language back
on itself.


We arrive from opposite directions, him from the Negative,
me from the Positive.
I sweat like Samuel Johnson
on pilgrimage.


I'm like a dictionary
thrown into
a blender.


He opens up
fresh desolation, the will
like a speck of vulture against the lapis lazuli of his cry.


Inspiral hunger
which devours itself
to the source!


This November I will be 33.
As if twice abandoned in Dante's
3rd Canto.


OoO? O!! Oooo….? His face
like a jellyfish
adrift in languagelessness.

According to the hermeneutics of the more extreme genetic
theorists, having transmitted my genes I am now of nil
significance, and can die.
I stick around, read Aquinas,
and revel in my monstrosity.


I read everyone: Milosz, Eckhart, Juan de san Matias,
Vallejo, Mandelstam, Celan, Popa, the author of The Cloud
of Unknowing, Plath, Hughes…
To take with me into the blank Lubianka
of the 21st Century.


Each eyeblink
cracks turquoise
afresh.


Ecce Homo! He declares,
with a spraycan
of raspberry.


He lies on his back, wriggling, as if
magnetised
to the Mysterium Tremendum.


When he cries, he bares
the hard rim
of his gums.


He hurtles into the long cold corridor of the world:
an emergency
ontologist.

At the gardens of Chatelhereult: showing to him the idiotexts
of unnamed flowers.
Our exile,
and home fires.


Bare road of the mind....
At the kerbside, this
blue flower.


Fuelled by the Absolute! Contingency's
fragile
engineering.

## About

Craig Coyle lives in Wishaw, and currently works as an Advanced Nurse Practitioner in Mental Health with NHS Lanarkshire. He has published in various magazines: Stand, Fire, Obsessed with Pipework, The English Chicago Review, Gutter, Verse, Poetry Salzburg, and Urthona. He was a mentee with the Clydebuilt Apprenticeship program in 2017. He has recently contributed to These Are The Hands, an anthology of poems celebrating the NHS, published by Fair Acre Press, proceeds from which go towards the Covid-19 emergency fund, and thereafter to NHS supported charities. His poem The Drive Home, selected from the anthology, was featured in The Guardian as Poem of the Month for April 2020.

Cover Illustration
Hildegard of Bingen: 'True Trinity in Unity' collage

Printed in Great Britain
by Amazon